Arranged by Mike Cramer

The following songs are the property of:
Bourne Co.
Music Publishers
5 West 37th Street
New York, NY 10018

BABY MINE
GIVE A LITTLE WHISTLE
HEIGH-HO
WHEN YOU WISH UPON A STAR
WHISTLE WHILE YOU WORK
WHO'S AFRAID OF THE BIG BAD WOLF?

ISBN 978-1-61780-385-7

Walt Disney Music Company
Wonderland Music Company, Inc.

7777 W. BLUEMOUND RD. P.O. BOX 13819 MILWAUKEE, WI 53213

Visit Hal Leonard Online at
www.halleonard.com

Contents

Baby Mine

from Walt Disney's DUMBO
Words by Ned Washington
Music by Frank Churchill

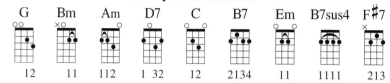

Verse
Moderately

1. Ba - by mine, don't you cry.
2. Lit - tle one, when you play,
3. From your head to your toes,

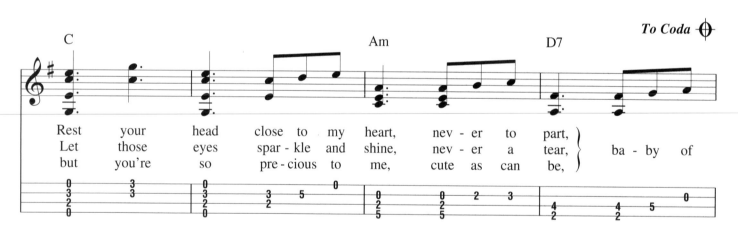

Ba - by mine, dry your eye.
don't you mind what they say.
you're not much good - ness knows,

To Coda ⊕

Rest your head close to my heart, nev - er to part,
Let those eyes spar - kle and shine, nev - er a tear,
but you're so pre - cious to me, cute as can be,

} ba - by of

mine.

Bridge

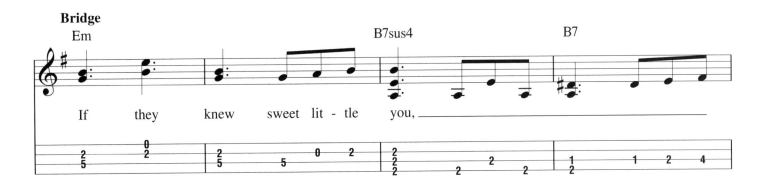

If they knew sweet lit - tle you,

they'd end up lov - ing you too.

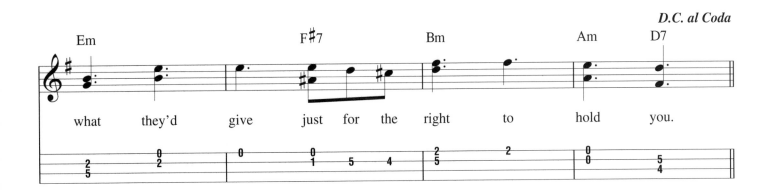

All those same peo - ple who scold you,

D.C. al Coda

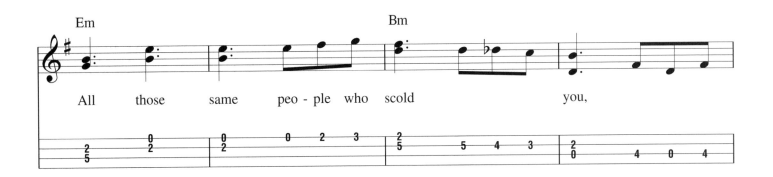

what they'd give just for the right to hold you.

Coda

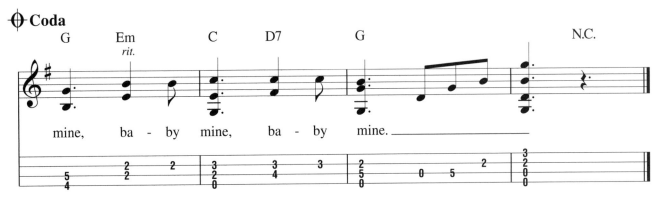

mine, ba - by mine, ba - by mine.

The Ballad of Davy Crockett

from Walt Disney's DAVY CROCKETT
Words by Tom Blackburn
Music by George Bruns

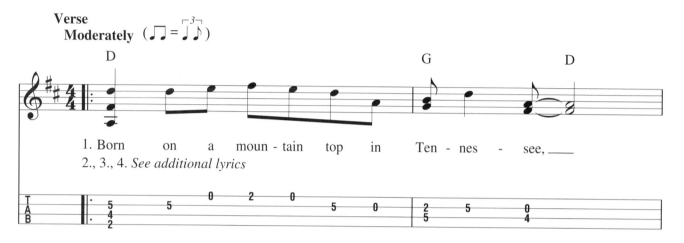

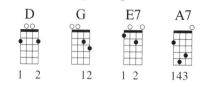

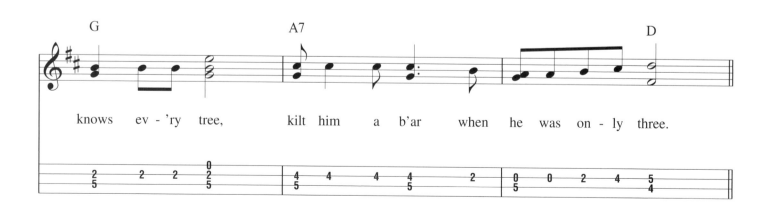

Chorus

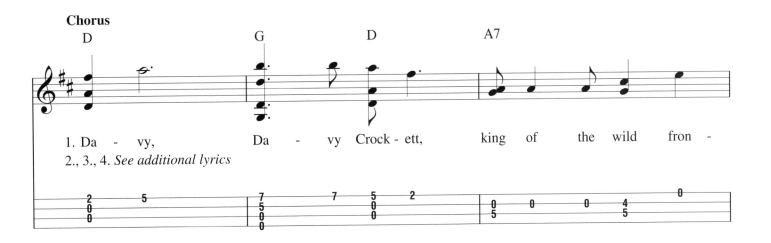

1. Da - vy, Da - vy Crock - ett, king of the wild fron -
2., 3., 4. *See additional lyrics*

1., 2., 3. tier!

4. **Slower** head - in' out West a - gain!

Additional Lyrics

Verse 2 Fought single-handed through the Injun War
Till the Creeks was whipped and peace was in store.
And while he was handlin' this risky chore
Made his-self a legend forevermore.

Chorus 2 Davy, Davy Crockett,
The man who don't know fear.

Verse 3 He went off to Congress and he served a spell
Fixin' up the government and laws as well.
Took over Washington so we heard tell
And patched up the crack in the Liberty Bell.

Chorus 3 Davy, Davy Crockett,
Seein' his duty clear.

Verse 4 When he'd come home, his politickin' done,
The western march had just begun.
So he packed his gear and his trusty gun,
And lit out a grinnin' to follow the sun.

Chorus 4 Davy, Davy Crockett,
Headin' out West again!

The Bare Necessities

from Walt Disney's THE JUNGLE BOOK

Words and Music by Terry Gilkyson

Chorus

Moderately fast

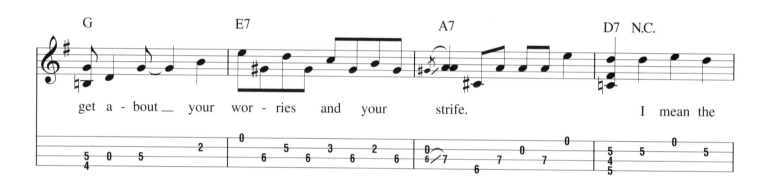

Look for the bare ne-ces-si-ties,_ the sim-ple bare ne-ces-si-ties;_ for-

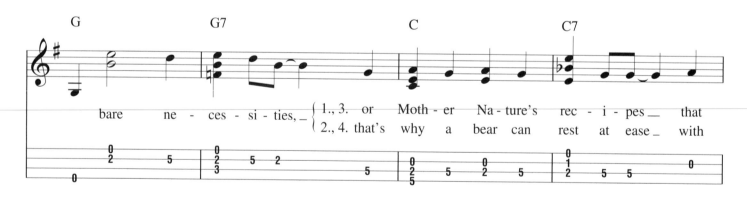

get a-bout_ your wor-ries and your strife. I mean the

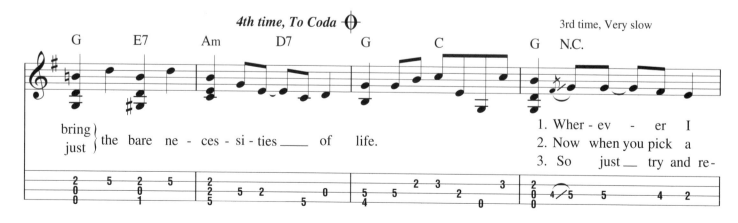

bare ne-ces-si-ties,_ { 1., 3. or Moth-er Na-ture's rec-i-pes_ that / 2., 4. that's why a bear can rest at ease_ with

4th time, To Coda ⊕   **3rd time, Very slow**

bring } / just } the bare ne-ces-si-ties ___ of life.

1. Wher-ev-er I
2. Now when you pick a
3. So just_ try and re-

Bridge

wan - der,   wher - ev - er I roam,
paw - paw   or a prick - ly pear;
lax   in my ___ back yard.

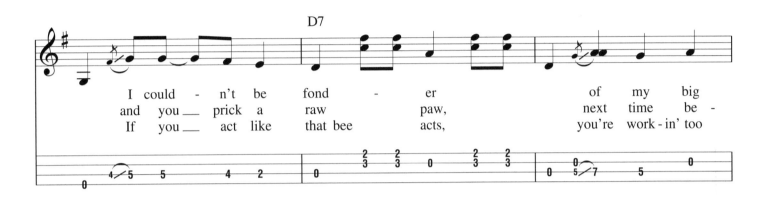

I could - n't be fond - er   of my big
and you ___ prick a raw paw,   next time be -
If you ___ act like that bee acts,   you're work - in' too

home.   The bees are buzz - in' in the
ware.   Don't pick the prick - ly pear by the
hard.   Don't spend your time just look - in' a -

3rd time, A tempo

tree to make _ some hon - ey just for me.   When
paw, when you pick a pear, try to use the claw.   But
round for some - thin' you want that can't be found.   When

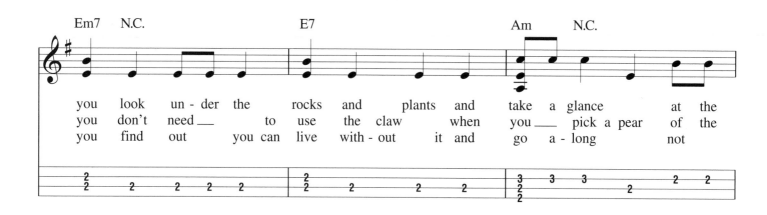

you look un - der the rocks and plants and take a glance at the
you don't need ___ to use the claw when you ___ pick a pear of the
you find out you can live with - out it and go a - long not

fan - cy ants, ___ then may - be ___ try a few.
big paw - paw. Have I giv - en you a clue?
think - in' a - bout ___ it. I'll tell you some - thin' true.

let ring

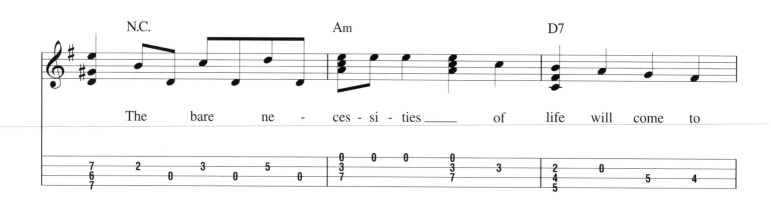

The bare ne - ces - si - ties ___ of life will come to

1., 2.

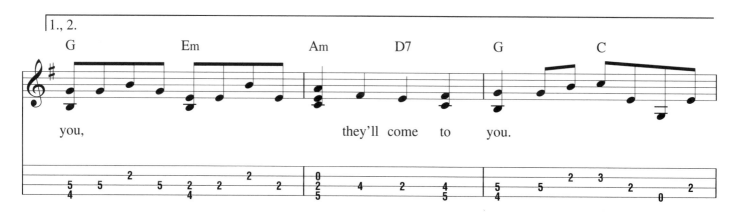

you, they'll come to you.

D.S. al Coda

$\oplus$ **Coda**

Outro-Tag

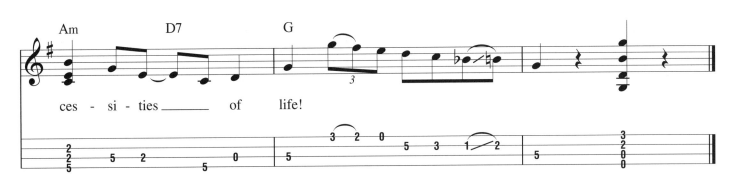

Be Our Guest

from Walt Disney's BEAUTY AND THE BEAST

Lyrics by Howard Ashman
Music by Alan Menken

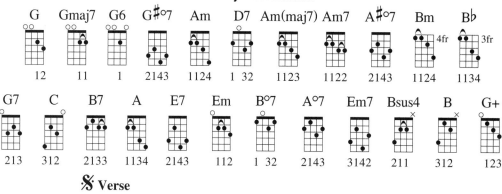

Verse

Moderately fast

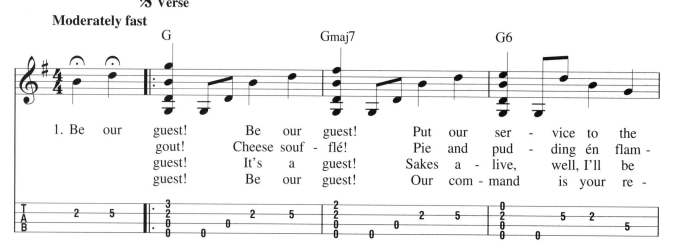

1. Be our guest! Be our guest! Put our ser - vice to the
   gout! Cheese souf - flé! Pie and pud - ding én flam -
   guest! It's a guest! Sakes a - live, well, I'll be
   guest! Be our guest! Our com - mand is your re -

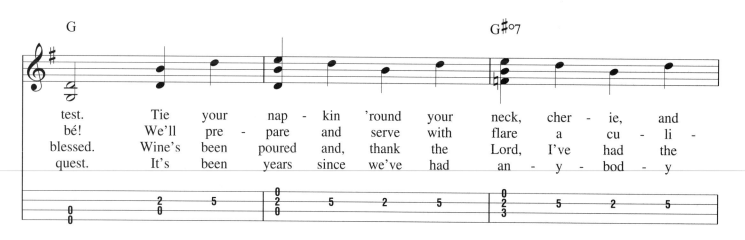

test. Tie your nap - kin 'round your neck, cher - ie, and
bé! We'll pre - pare and serve with flare a cu - li -
blessed. Wine's been poured and, thank the Lord, I've had the
quest. It's been years since we've had an - y - bod - y

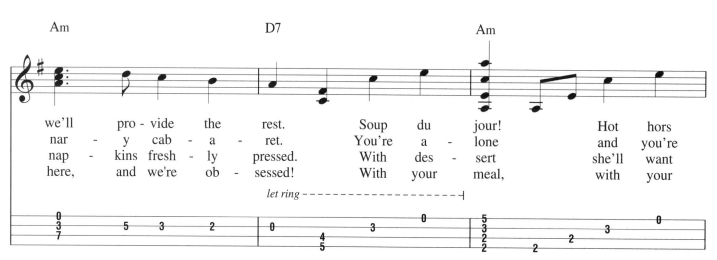

we'll pro - vide the rest. Soup du jour! Hot hors
nar - y cab - a - ret. You're a - lone and you're
nap - kins fresh - ly pressed. With des - sert she'll want
here, and we're ob - sessed! With your meal, with your

let ring - - - - - - - - - - - - - - - - - - -

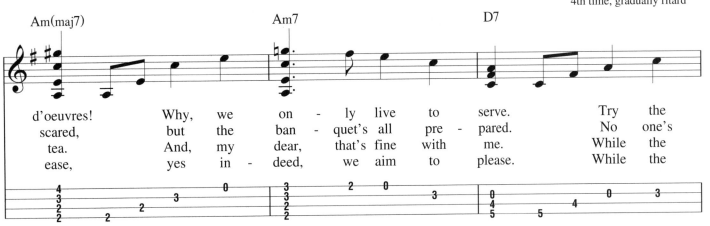

d'oeuvres! Why, we on - ly live to serve. Try the
scared, but the ban - quet's all pre - pared. No one's
tea. And, my dear, that's fine with me. While the
ease, yes in - deed, we aim to please. While the

4th time, To Coda 1

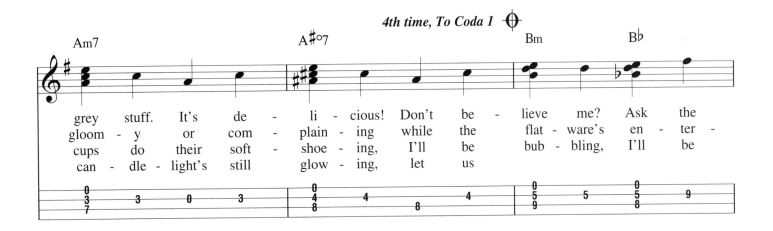

grey stuff. It's de - li - cious! Don't be - lieve me? Ask the
gloom - y or com - plain - ing while the flat - ware's en - ter -
cups do their soft - shoe - ing, I'll be bub - bling, I'll be
can - dle - light's still glow - ing, let us

4th time, Very slow & gradually accelerate

dish - es! They can sing! They can dance! Af - ter
tain - ing. We tell jokes! I can do tricks with my
brew - ing. I'll get warm, pip - ing hot. Heav - en's
course, one by one, 'til you

all, Miss, this is France! And a din - ner here is
fel - low can - dle - sticks. And it's all in per - fect
sake, is that a spot? Clean it up! We want the
shout: "E - nough! I'm done!" Then we'll sing you off to

G7   C   B7

nev - er sec - ond best.   Go on, un - fold your men -
taste. That, you can bet.   Come on and lift your glass. __
com - pa - ny im - pressed.   We've got a lot to do! __
sleep as you di - gest.   To - night you'll prop your feet __

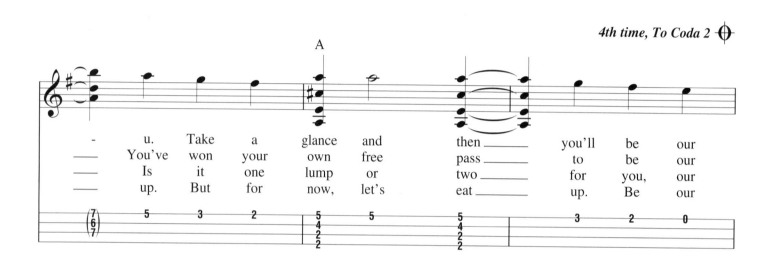

4th time, To Coda 2 ⊕

A

- u. Take a glance and   then __ you'll be our
__ You've won your own and free   pass __ to be our
__ Is it one lump or   two __ for you, our
__ up. But for now, let's   eat __ up. Be our

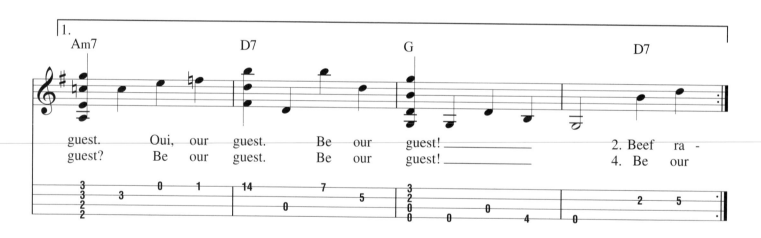

1.

Am7   D7   G   D7

guest. Oui, our guest. Be our guest! __ 2. Beef ra -
guest? Be our guest. Be our guest! __ 4. Be our

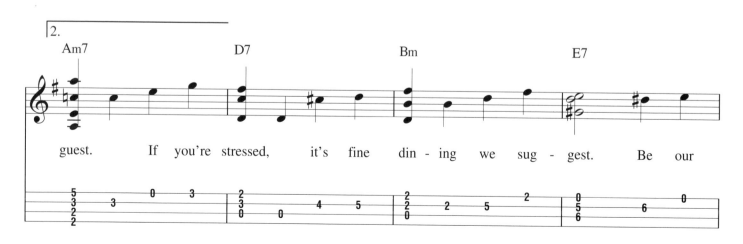

2.

Am7   D7   Bm   E7

guest. If you're stressed, it's fine din - ing we sug - gest. Be our

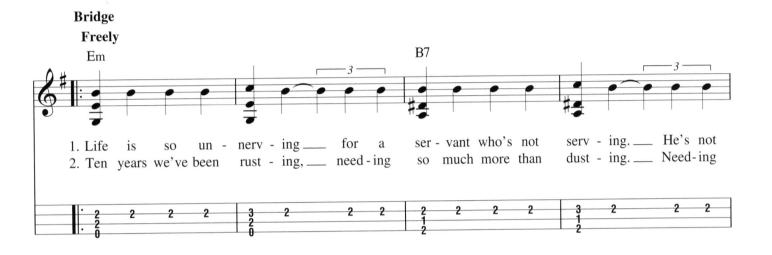

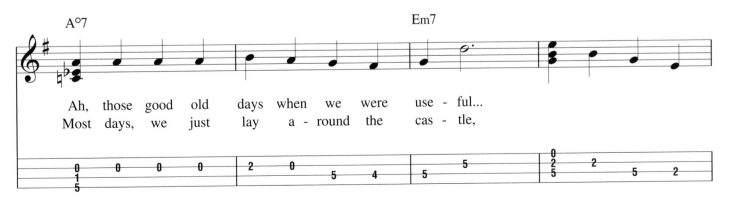

Circle of Life

from Walt Disney Pictures' THE LION KING

Music by Elton John
Lyrics by Tim Rice

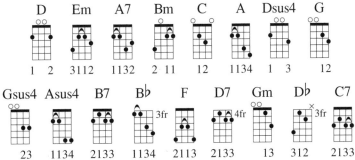

sun roll-ing high _____ through the sap - phi - re sky _ keeps great and small _ on the end - less _

let ring - - - - ⌐   *let ring - - - - - - - - - - - - - - - - - ⌐*

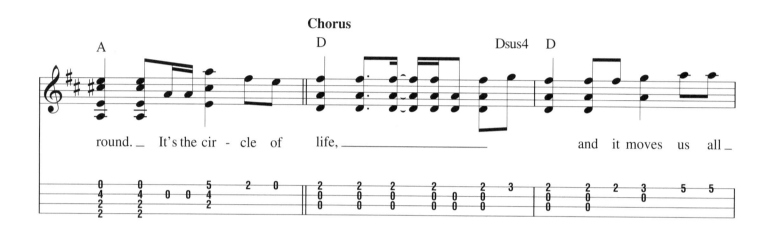

Chorus

round. _ It's the cir - cle of life, _____ and it moves us all _

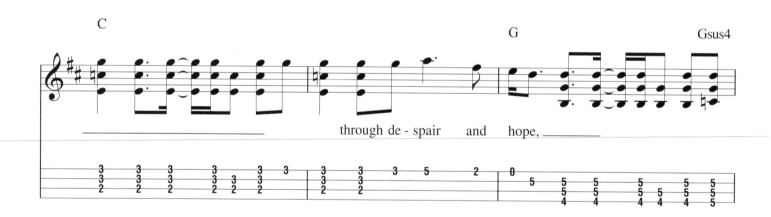

_____ through de - spair and hope, ____

through faith and _ love,   'til we find our place _

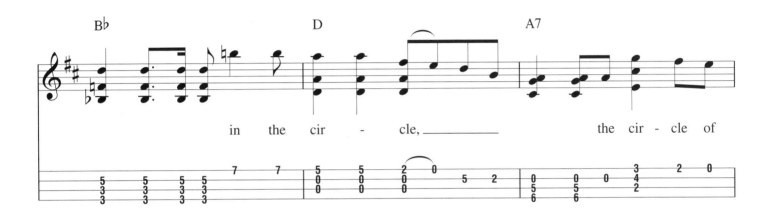

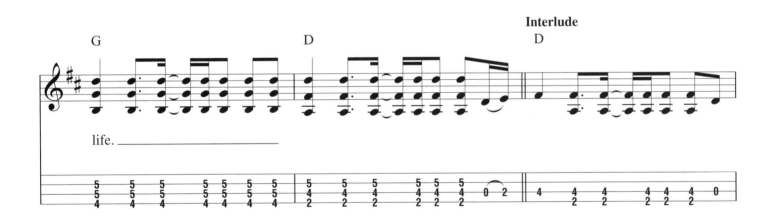

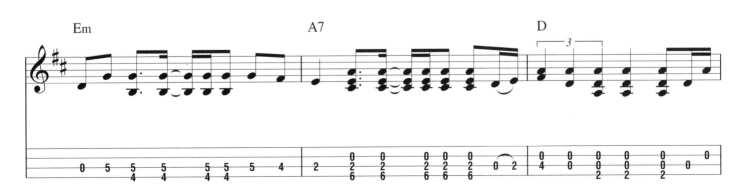

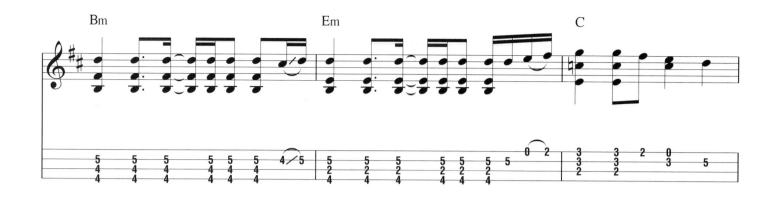

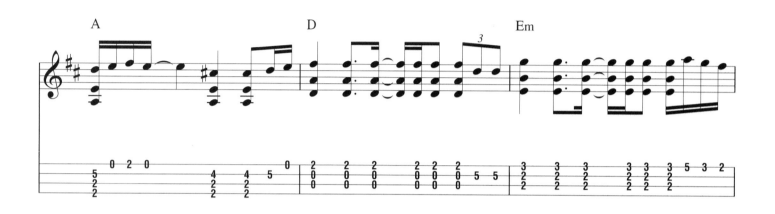

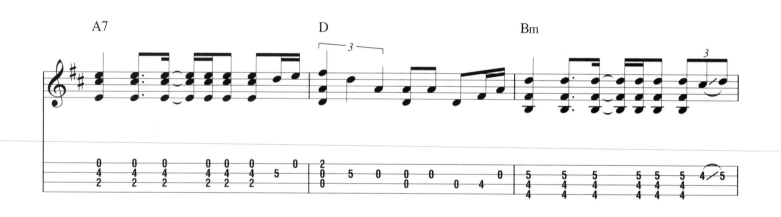

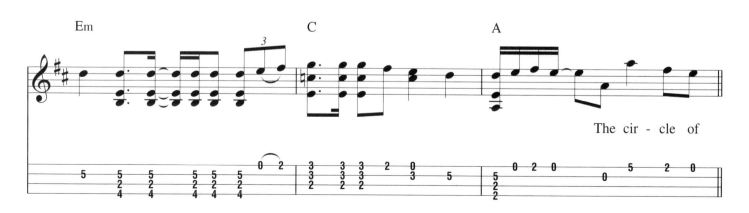

The cir - cle of

Bella Notte
(This Is the Night)

from Walt Disney's LADY AND THE TRAMP
Words and Music by Peggy Lee and Sonny Burke

Bibbidi-Bobbidi-Boo
(The Magic Song)

from Walt Disney's CINDERELLA

Words by Jerry Livingston
Music by Mack David and Al Hoffman

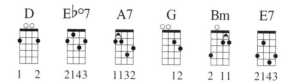

Verse
Moderately

1., 2. Sa - la - ga - doo - la, men - chic - ka boo - la, bib - bi - di - bob - bi - di -

boo.

{ Put 'em to - geth - er and what have you got? }
{ It - 'll do mag - ic, be - lieve it or not. }

Bib - bi - di - bob - bi - di - boo.   boo.   Now,

Chim Chim Cher-ee

from Walt Disney's MARY POPPINS

Words and Music by Richard M. Sherman and Robert B. Sherman

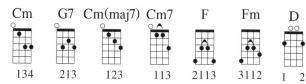

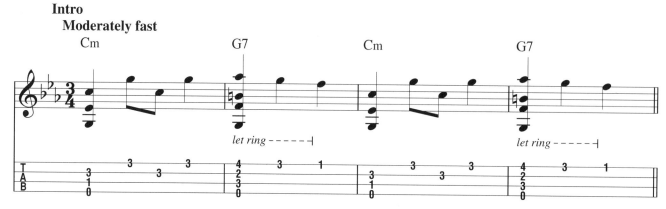

Intro
Moderately fast

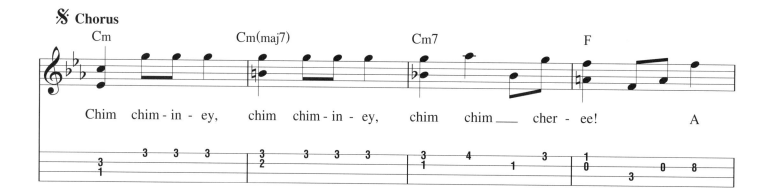

Chorus

Chim chim-in-ey, chim chim-in-ey, chim chim ___ cher-ee! A

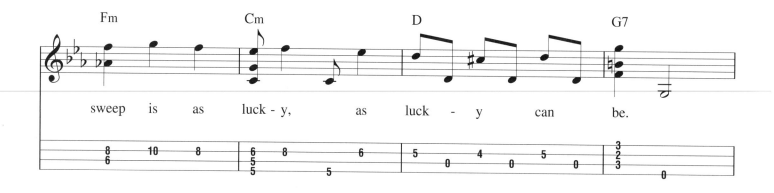

sweep is as luck-y, as luck-y can be.

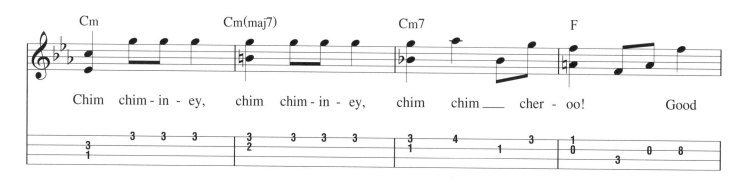

Chim chim-in-ey, chim chim-in-ey, chim chim ___ cher-oo! Good

Interlude

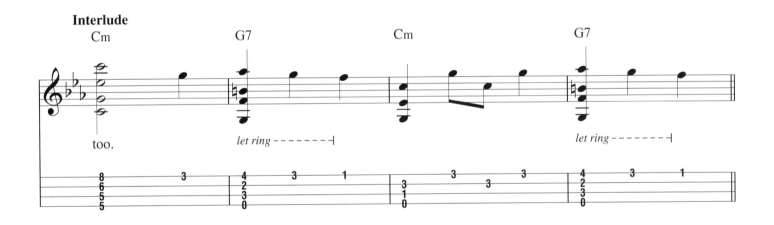

Verse

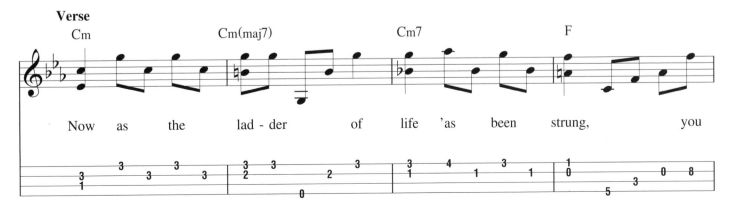

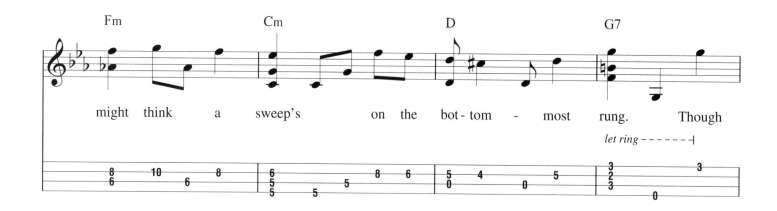

might think a sweep's on the bot-tom - most rung. Though

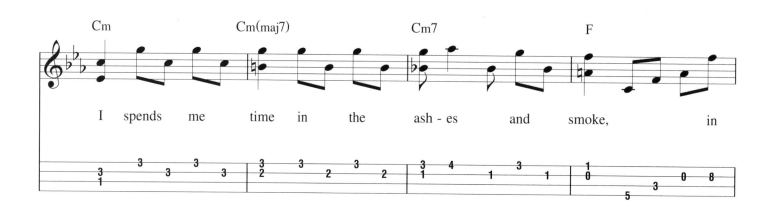

I spends me time in the ash - es and smoke, in

D.S. al Coda

this 'ole wide world there's no 'ap - pi - er bloke.

⊕ Coda

Chorus

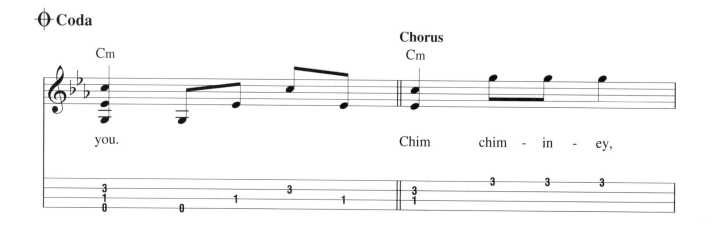

you.   Chim chim - in - ey,

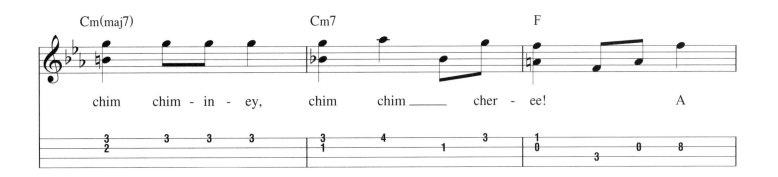

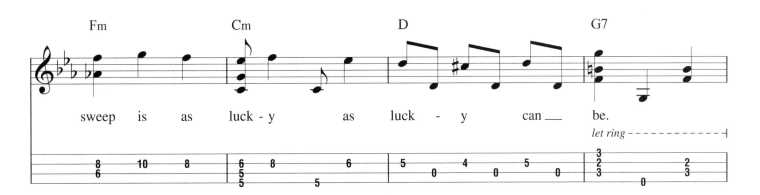

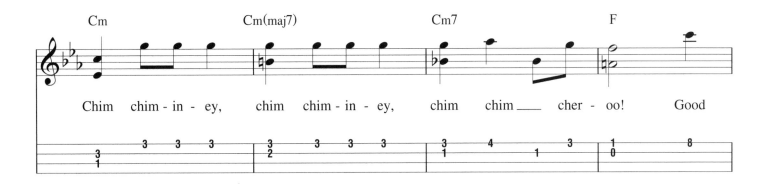

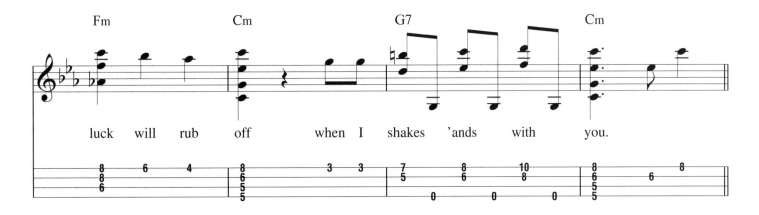

Outro-Tag

Colors of the Wind

from Walt Disney's POCAHONTAS

Music by Alan Menken
Lyrics by Stephen Schwartz

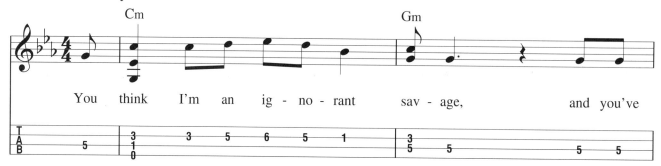

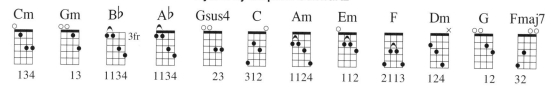

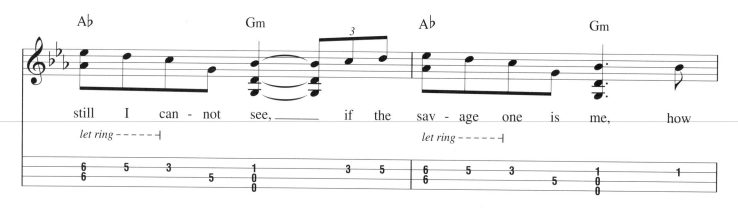

Interlude
A tempo

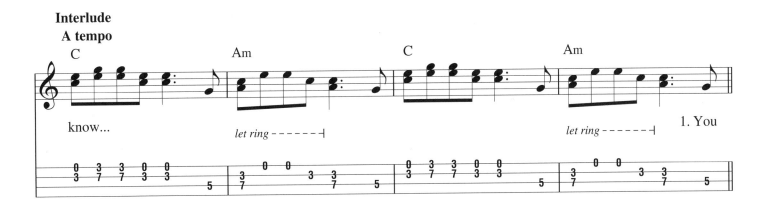

know...   *let ring - - - - - -⌐*   *let ring - - - - - -⌐*   1. You

𝄋 Verse

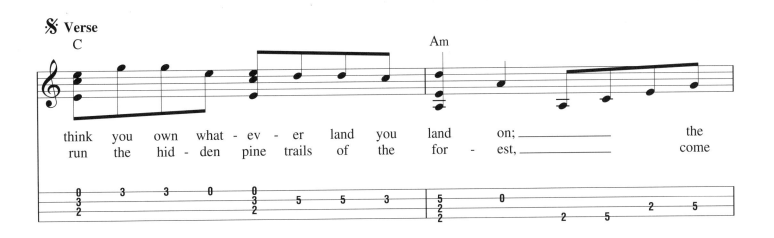

think   you   own   what - ev - er   land   you   land   on; _____   the
run   the   hid - den   pine   trails   of   the   for - est, _____   come

earth   is   just   a   dead   thing   you   can   claim; _____   but
taste   the   sun - sweet   ber - ries   of   the   earth; _____   come

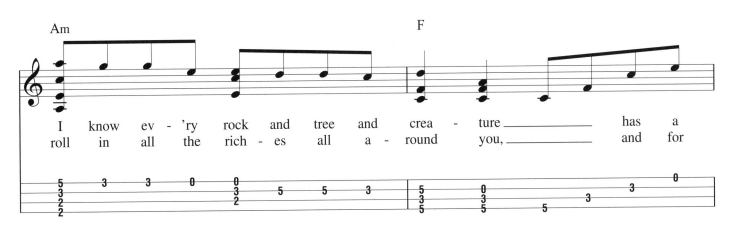

I   know   ev - 'ry   rock   and   tree   and   crea - ture _____   has   a
roll   in   all   the   rich - es   all   a - round   you, _____   and   for

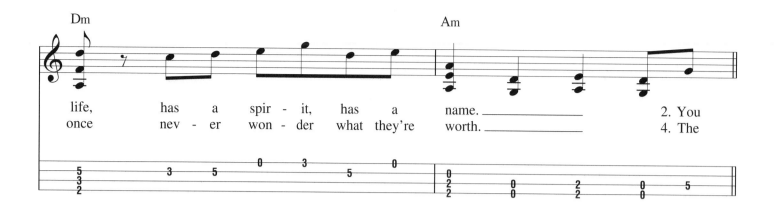

life,   has   a   spir - it,   has   a   name. _____   2. You
once   nev - er   won - der   what they're   worth. _____   4. The

Verse

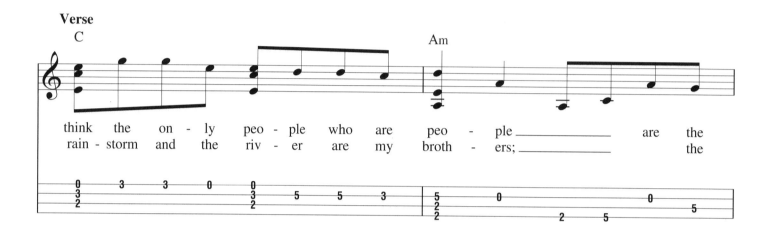

think   the   on - ly   peo - ple   who   are   peo -   ple _____   are   the
rain - storm and   the   riv - er   are   my   broth -   ers; _____   the

peo -   ple   who   look   and   think   like   you, _____   but
her -   on   and   the   ot -   ter   are   my   friends, _____   and

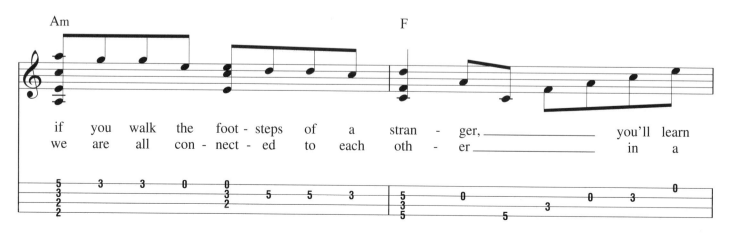

if   you   walk   the   foot - steps   of   a   stran - ger, _____   you'll learn
we   are   all   con - nect - ed   to   each   oth -   er _____   in   a

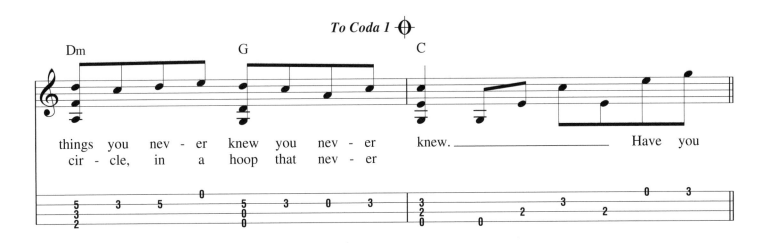

things you nev - er knew you nev - er knew. _____ Have you

cir - cle, in a hoop that nev - er

𝄋 𝄋 Chorus

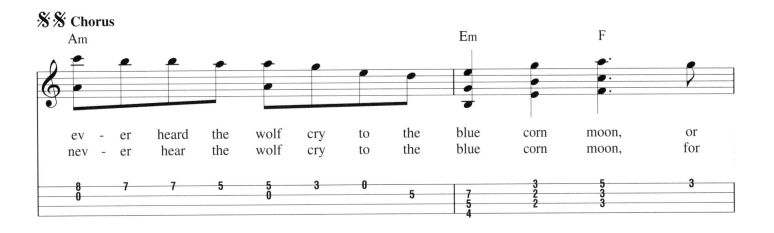

ev - er heard the wolf cry to the blue corn moon, or

nev - er hear the wolf cry to the blue corn moon, for

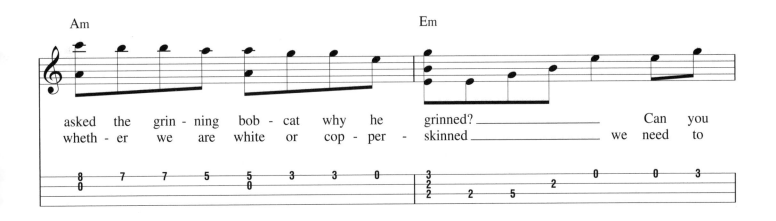

asked the grin - ning bob - cat why he grinned? _____ Can you

wheth - er we are white or cop - per - skinned _____ we need to

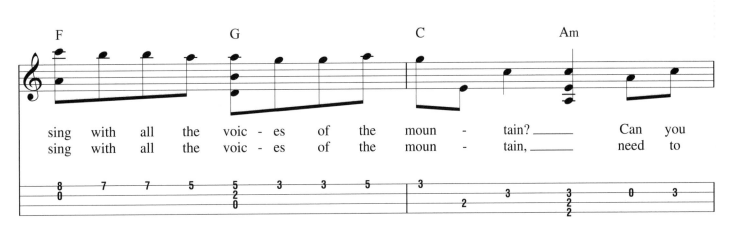

sing with all the voic - es of the moun - tain? _____ Can you

sing with all the voic - es of the moun - tain, _____ need to

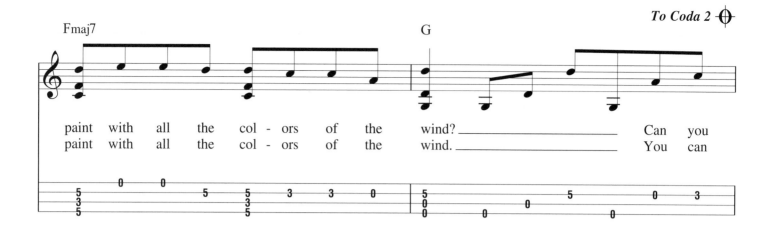

paint with all the col - ors of the wind? _____ Can you
paint with all the col - ors of the wind. _____ You can

Interlude
A tempo

paint with all the col - ors of the wind?

D.S. al Coda 1

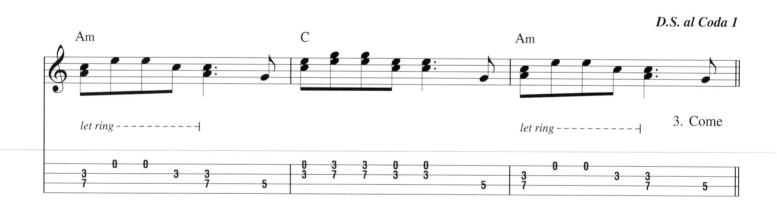

3. Come

Coda 1

Bridge

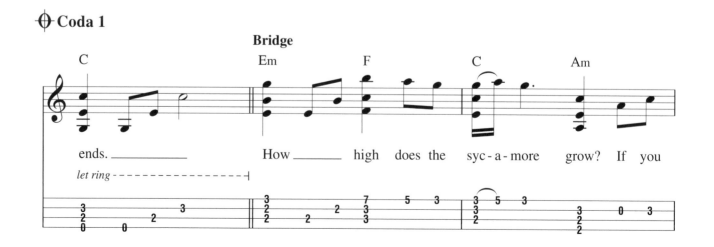

ends. _____ How _____ high does the syc - a - more grow? If you

cut it down, _____ then you'll nev - er know. _____ And you'll

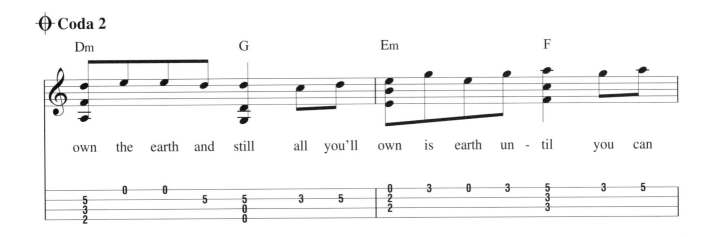

⊕ Coda 2

own the earth and still all you'll own is earth un - til you can

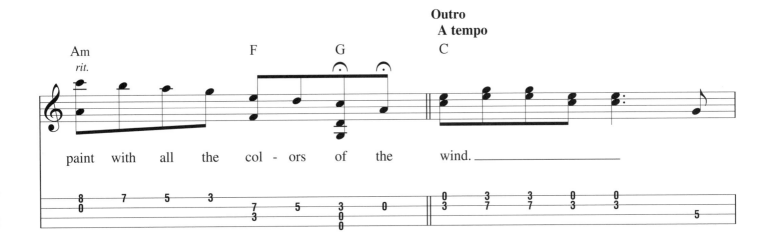

Outro
A tempo

paint with all the col - ors of the wind. _____

Give a Little Whistle

from Walt Disney's PINOCCHIO
Words by Ned Washington
Music by Leigh Harline

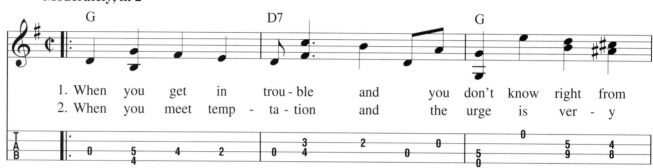

Verse
Moderately, in 2

1. When you get in trou-ble and you don't know right from
2. When you meet temp-ta-tion and the urge is ver-y

wrong: } give a lit-tle whis-tle,   *Whistle:* ------   give a lit-tle
strong: }   *let ring* ---------

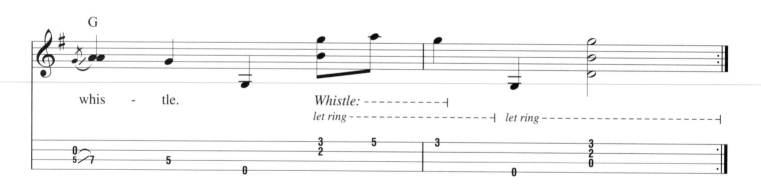

whis - tle.   *Whistle:* -----------
               let ring -------------   *let ring* ------------------

Bridge

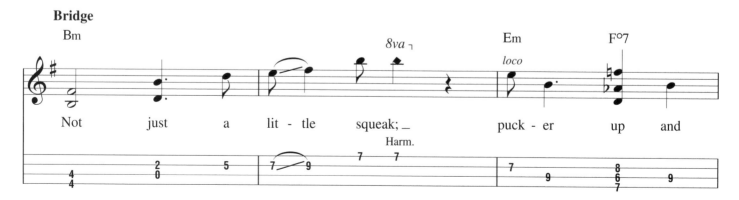

Not   just   a lit-tle   squeak;   puck-er   up   and
               Harm.

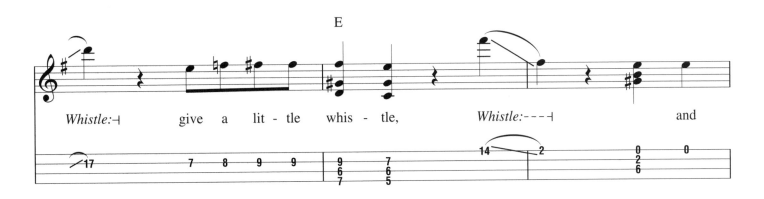

Go the Distance

from Walt Disney Pictures' HERCULES

Music by Alan Menken
Lyrics by David Zippel

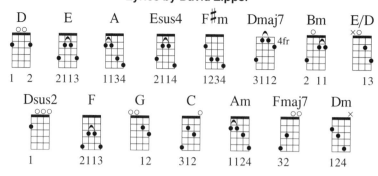

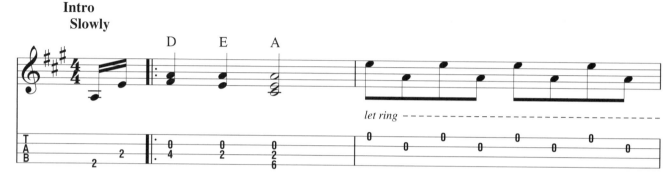

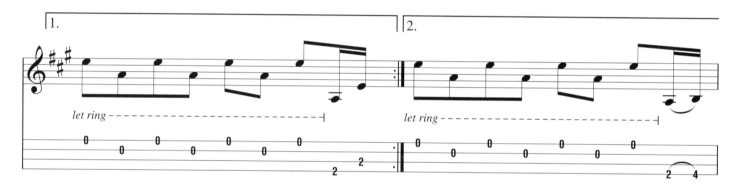

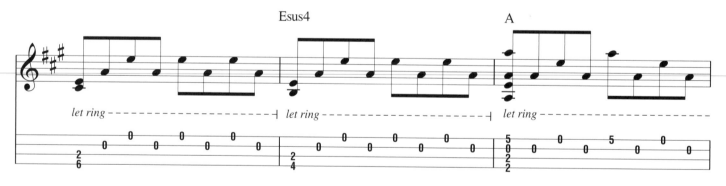

I have of-ten dreamed_ of a far-off place _ where a

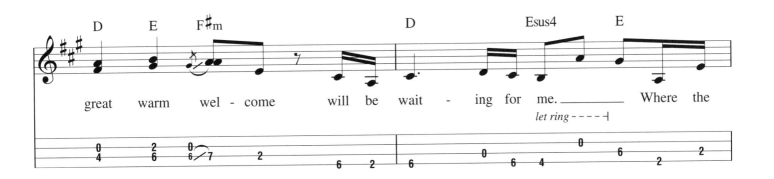

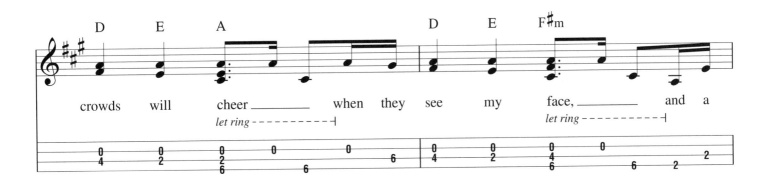

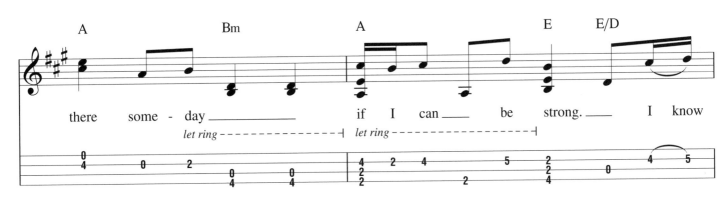

ev - 'ry mile   will be   worth   my __ while. ___   I would

go   most   an - y - where   to   feel   like   I _____   be -

Interlude

long. _____

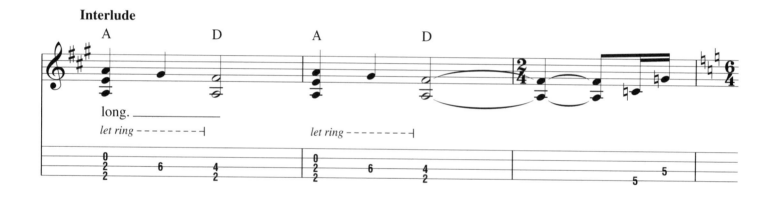

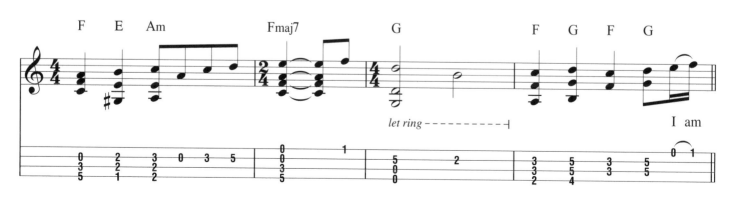

I am

He's a Tramp

from Walt Disney's LADY AND THE TRAMP
Words and Music by Peggy Lee and Sonny Burke

Verse

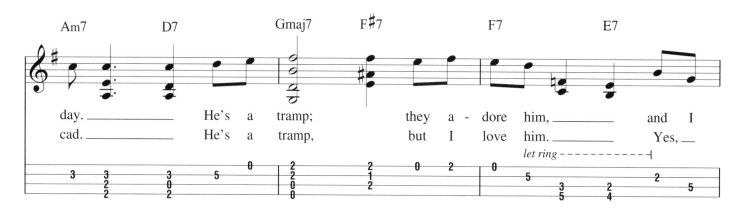

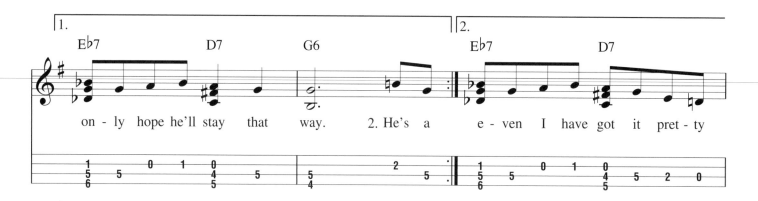

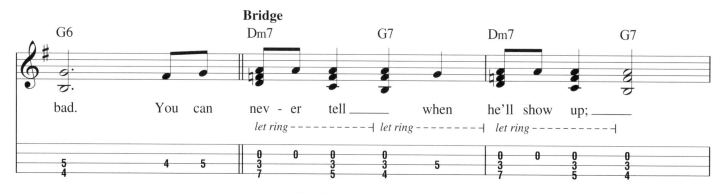

Heigh-Ho

The Dwarfs' Marching Song from Walt Disney's SNOW WHITE AND THE SEVEN DWARFS

Words by Larry Morey
Music by Frank Churchill

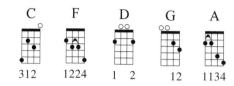

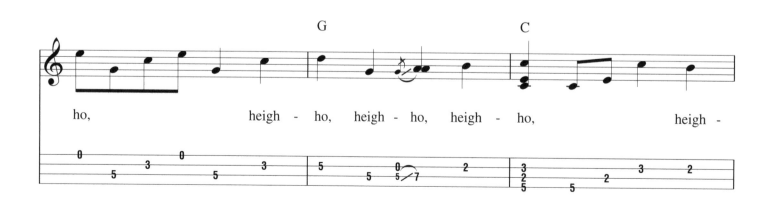

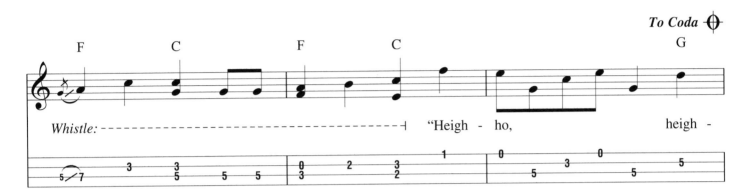

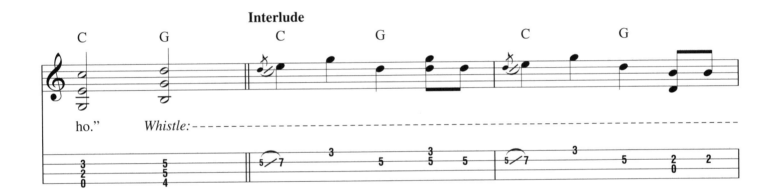

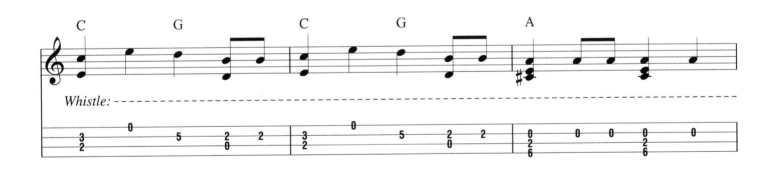

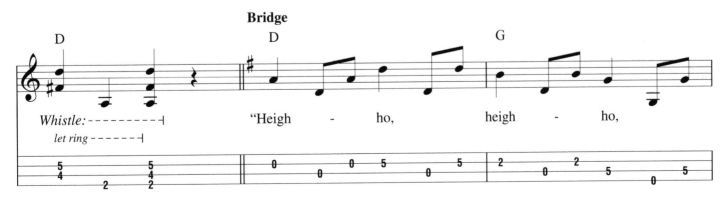

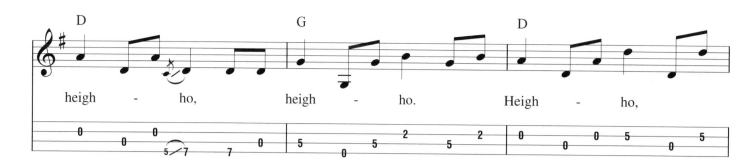

heigh - ho, heigh - ho. Heigh - ho,

D.S. al Coda

heigh - ho, heigh - ho, hum." "Heigh -

Coda

ho. Heigh - ho, heigh - ho," it's

home from work we go. *Whistle:* -

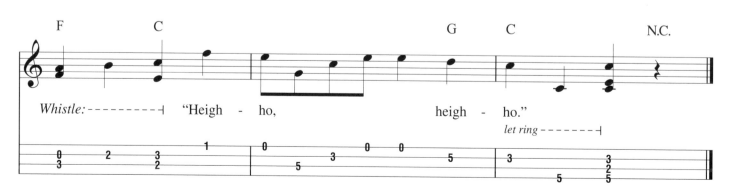

Whistle: - - - - - - - - | "Heigh - ho, heigh - ho."

let ring - - - - - - - - |

A Spoonful of Sugar

from Walt Disney's MARY POPPINS
Words and Music by Richard M. Sherman and Robert B. Sherman

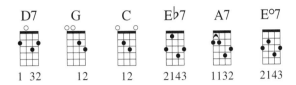

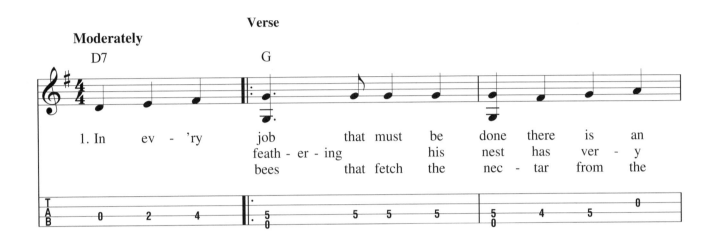

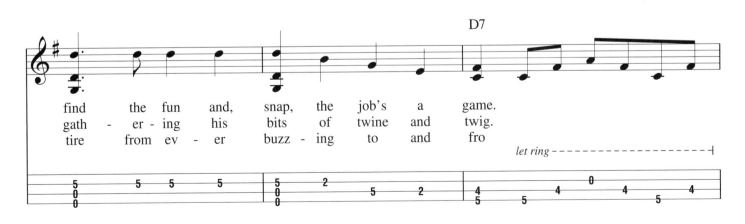

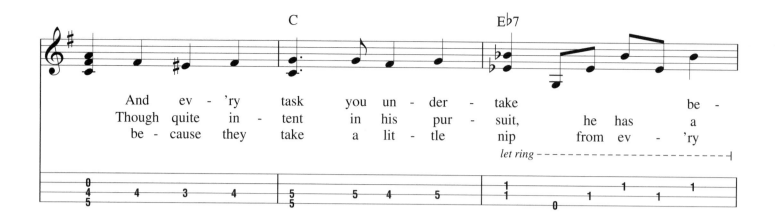

And ev - 'ry task you un - der - take be -
Though quite in - tent in his pur - suit, he has a
be - cause they take a lit - tle nip from ev - 'ry

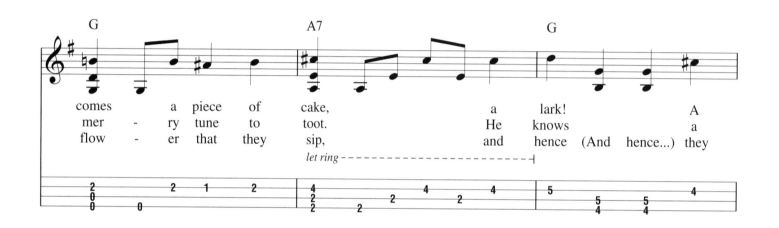

comes a piece of cake, a lark! A
mer - ry tune to toot. He knows a
flow - er that they sip, and hence (And hence...) they

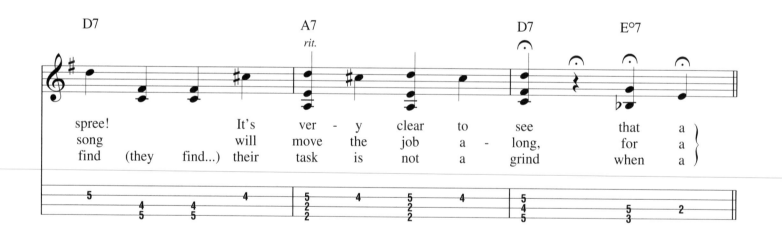

spree! It's ver - y clear to see that a
song will move the job a - long, for a
find (they find...) their task is not a grind when a

Chorus
A tempo

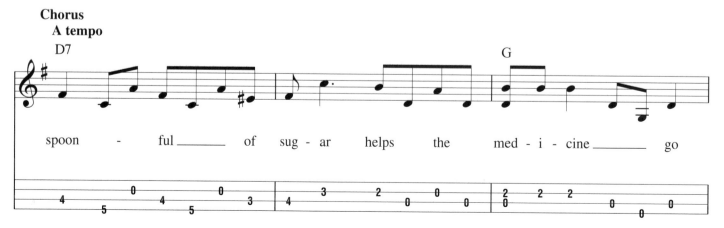

spoon - ful _____ of sug - ar helps the med - i - cine _____ go

down,   the med - i - cine _____ go   down, _____

med - i - cine   go   down.   Just   a   spoon - ful _____ of

sug - ar   helps   the   med - i - cine _____ go   down _____

in   a   most de - light - ful   way. _____

2. A   rob - in   way. _____
3. The   hon - ey -

It's a Small World

from Disneyland Resort® and Magic Kingdom® Park

Words and Music by Richard M. Sherman and Robert B. Sherman

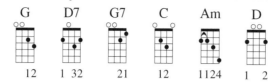

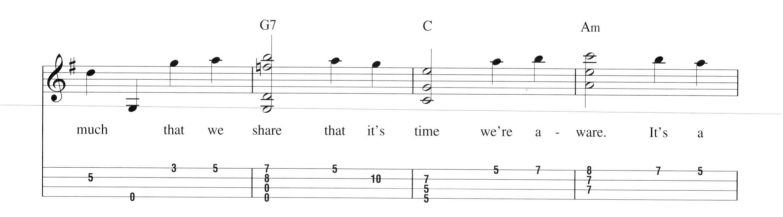

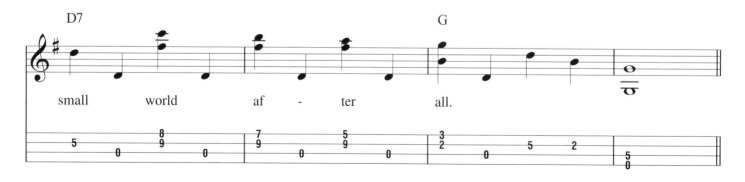

Chorus

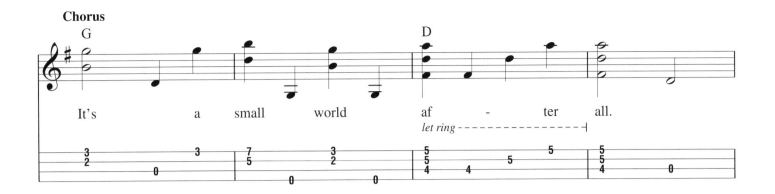

It's   a   small   world   af - ter   all.

let ring

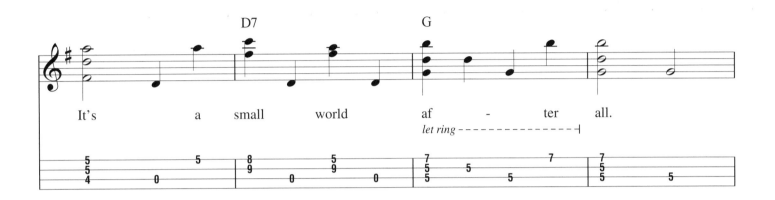

It's   a   small   world   af - ter   all.

let ring

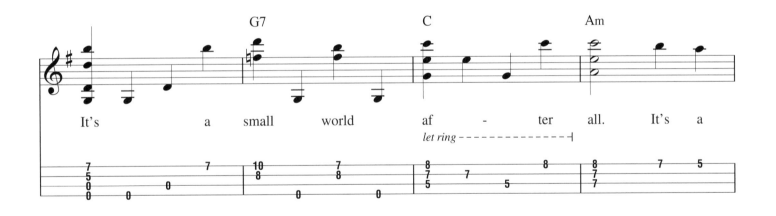

It's   a   small   world   af - ter   all.   It's   a

let ring

small,   small   world.   It's   a

let ring ---------   *let ring* ---------

1.   2.

Mickey Mouse March

from Walt Disney's THE MICKEY MOUSE CLUB
Words and Music by Jimmie Dodd

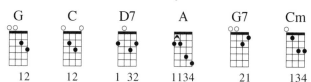

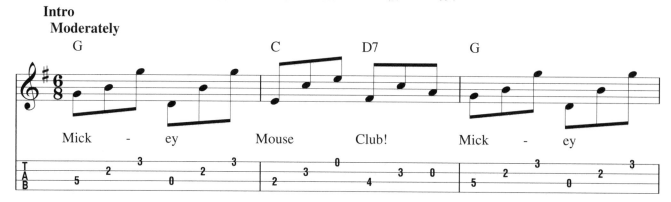

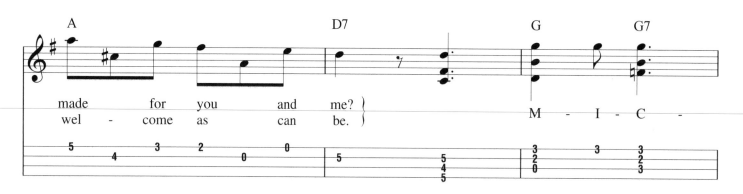

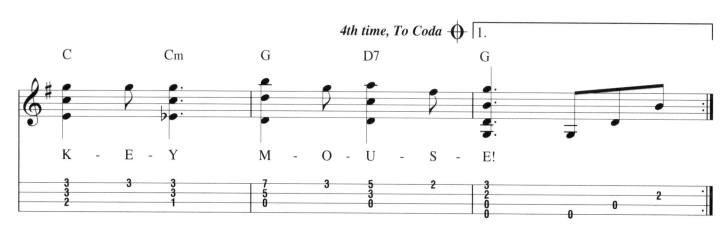

Shrimp Boats

Words and Music by Paul Mason Howard and Paul Weston

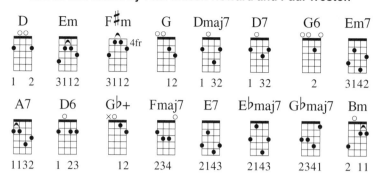

Intro
Moderately

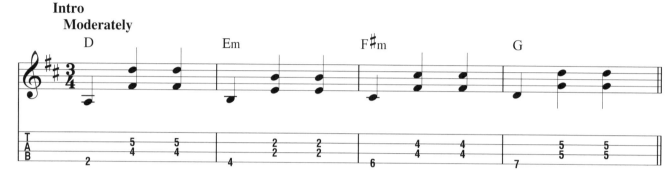

Chorus

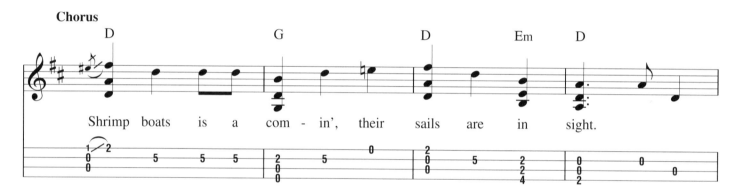

Shrimp boats is a com-in', their sails are in sight.

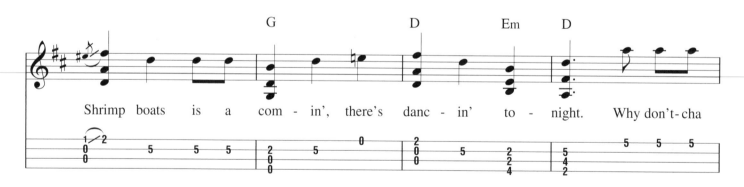

Shrimp boats is a com-in', there's danc-in' to-night. Why don't-cha

hur-ry, hur-ry, hur-ry home, why don't-cha hur-ry, hur-ry, hur-ry home? Look, here the

let ring - - - - - - - -   *let ring - - - - - - - -*

Supercalifragilisticexpialidocious

from Walt Disney's MARY POPPINS

Words and Music by Richard M. Sherman and Robert B. Sherman

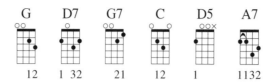

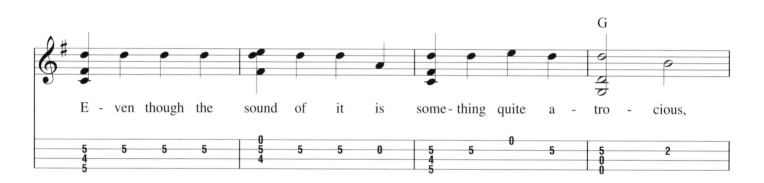

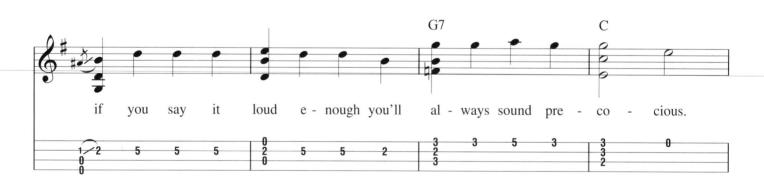

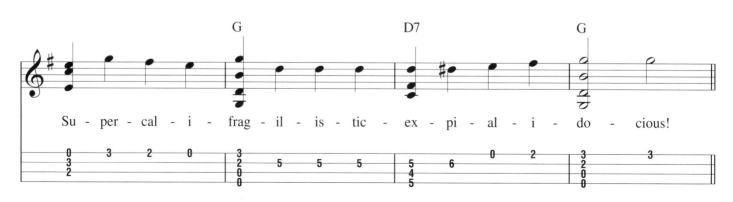

Bridge

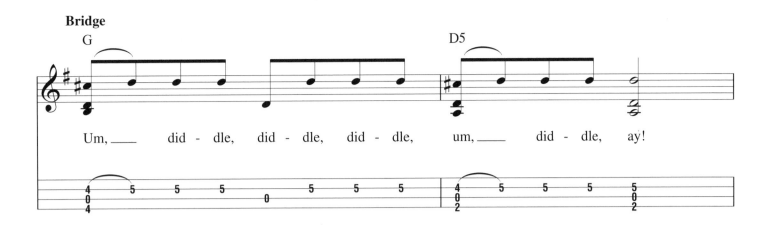

Um, ___ did - dle, did - dle, did - dle, um, ___ did - dle, ay!

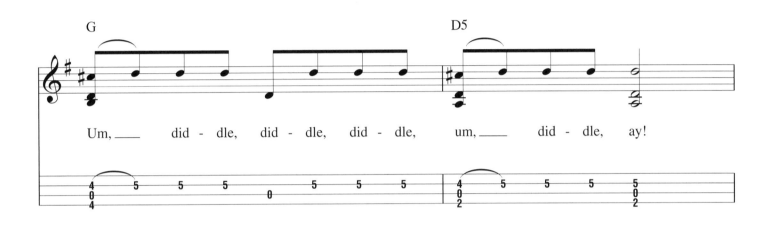

Um, ___ did - dle, did - dle, did - dle, um, ___ did - dle, ay!

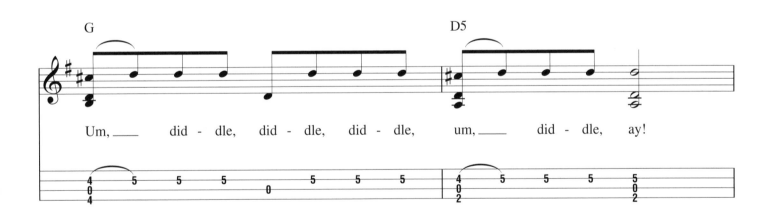

Um, ___ did - dle, did - dle, did - dle, um, ___ did - dle, ay!

Um, ___ did - dle, did - dle, did - dle, um, ___ did - dle, ay!
1. Be -
2. He
3. So

Verse

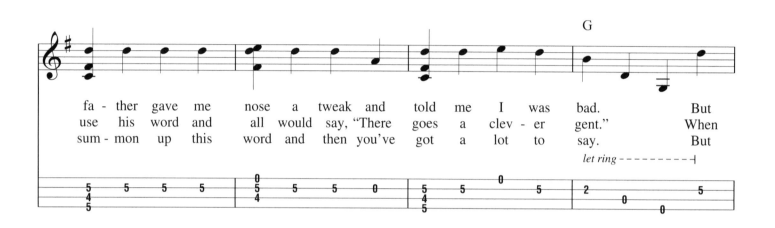

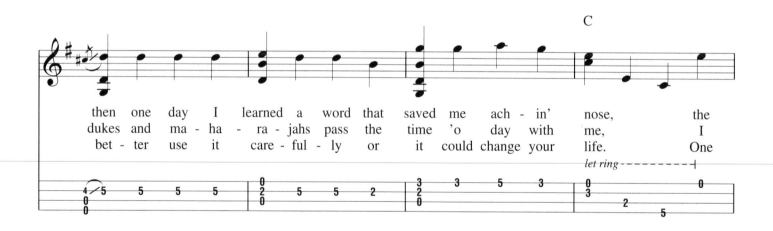

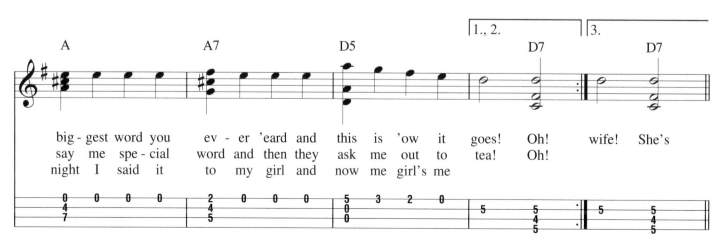

60

Chorus
Faster

su - per - cal - i - frag - il - is - tic - ex - pi - al - i - do - cious!

Su - per - cal - i - frag - il - is - tic - ex - pi - al - i - do - cious!

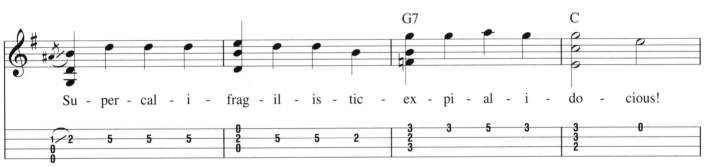

Su - per - cal - i - frag - il - is - tic - ex - pi - al - i - do - cious!

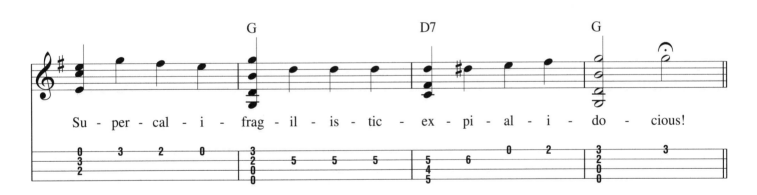

Su - per - cal - i - frag - il - is - tic - ex - pi - al - i - do - cious!

Outro-Tag
Very fast

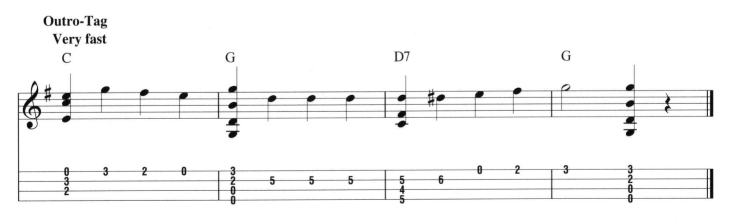

Under the Sea

from Walt Disney's THE LITTLE MERMAID

Music by Alan Menken
Lyrics by Howard Ashman

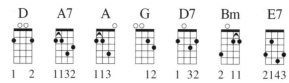

Intro
Moderately, in 2

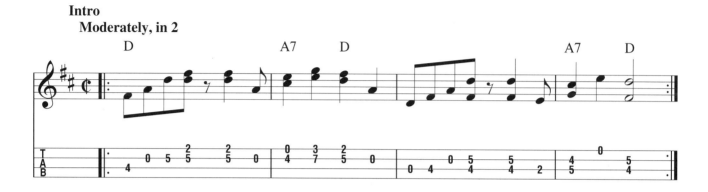

Verse

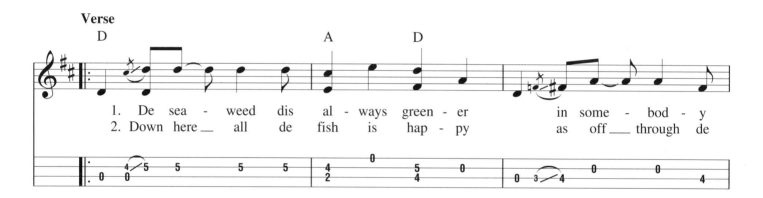

1. De sea - weed dis al - ways green - er in some - bod - y
2. Down here ___ all de fish is hap - py as off ___ through de

else - 's lake. You dream ___ a - bout go - ing up dere,
waves dey roll. De fish ___ on de land ain't hap - py.

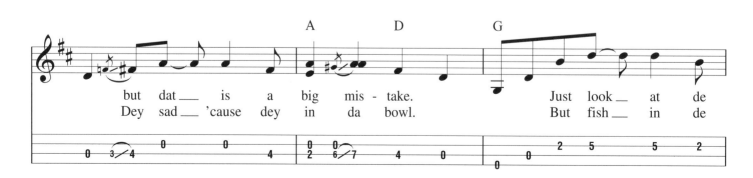

but dat ___ is a big mis - take. Just look ___ at de
Dey sad ___ 'cause dey in da bowl. But fish ___ in de

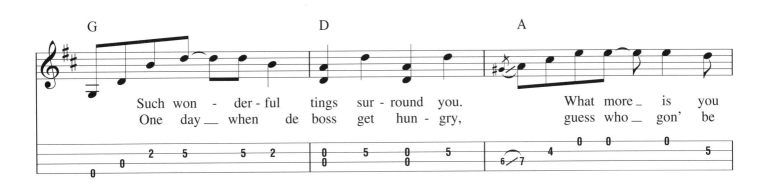

Chorus

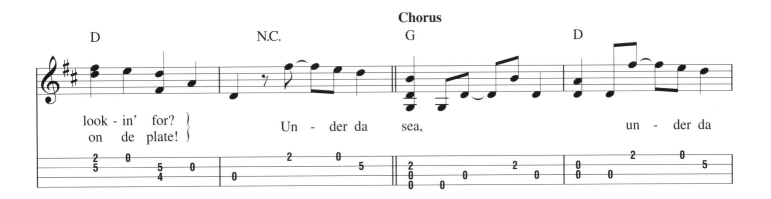

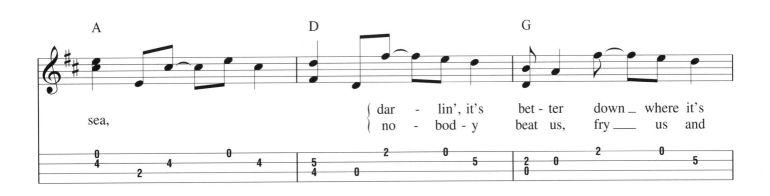

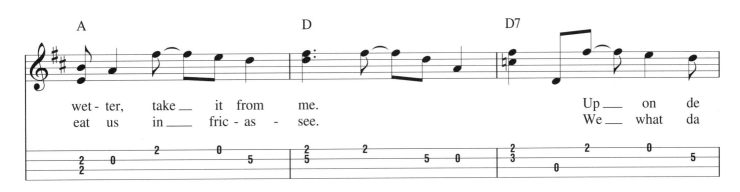

shore dey work __ all day. __ Out __ in de sun dey slave __ a - way __
land folks loves __ to cook. __ Un - der da sea, we off __ da hook. __

__ while __ we de - vot - in' full __ time to float - in' } un - der da
__ We __ got no troub - les, life __ is de bub - bles } un - der da

1.

Interlude

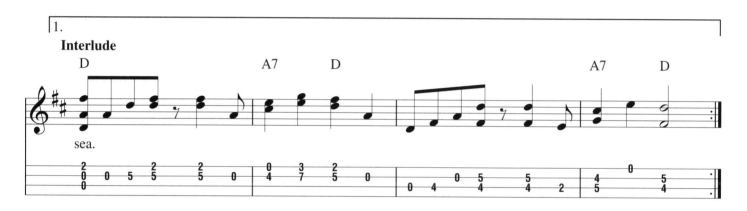

sea.

2.

𝄋 **Chorus**

sea, __ un - der da sea.
(Un - der __ da sea. __ Un - der __ da sea.)

Since __ life is sweet here, we __ got de beat here nat - u - ral -
When __ de sar - dine be - gin __ de be - guine, it's mu - sic to

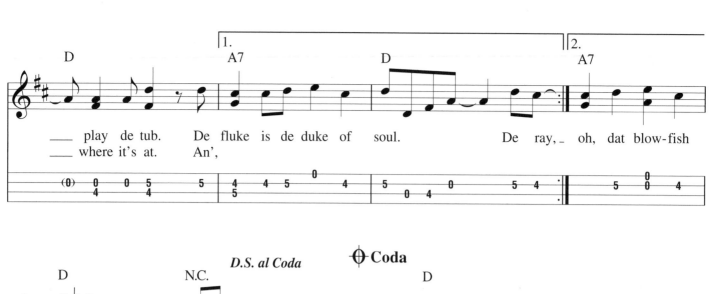

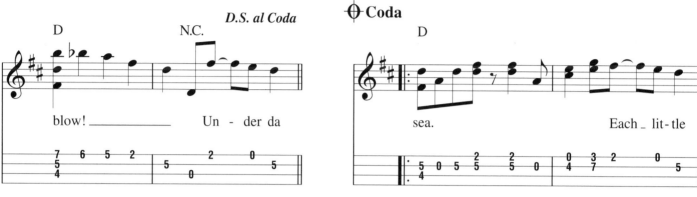

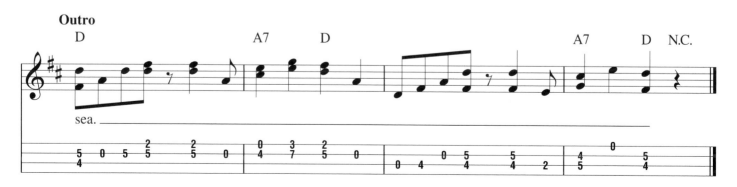

Westward Ho, the Wagons!

from Walt Disney's WESTWARD HO, THE WAGONS!

Words by Tom Blackburn
Music by George Bruns

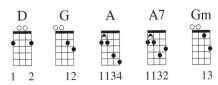

Intro
Slowly

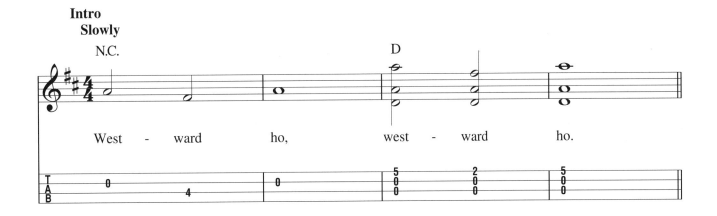

West - ward ho, west - ward ho.

Lively

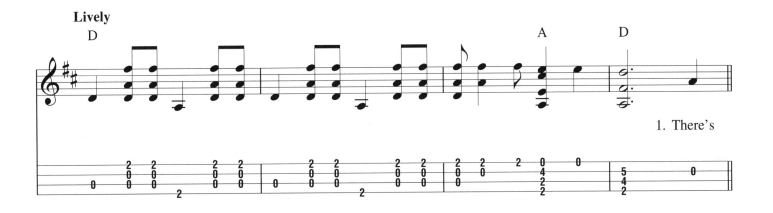

1. There's

℞ **Verse**

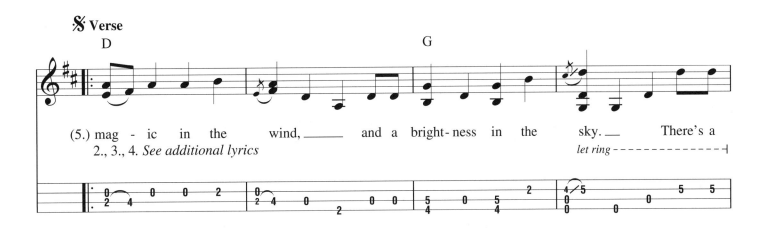

(5.) mag - ic in the wind, _____ and a bright-ness in the sky. _____ There's a
2., 3., 4. *See additional lyrics*
let ring - - - - - - - - - - - - -

prom - ised land a - wait - in' and we'll get there bye and bye. _____ West - ward

Chorus

1., 4. ho, _____ the wag - ons! Al - ways west - ward
2., 3., 5. roll _____ the wag - ons, west - ward roll _____ 'em

roll. _____ West - ward ho, _____ the wag - ons,
far. _____ West - ward roll _____ the wag - ons

5th time, To Coda ⊕

Or - e - gon's our _____ goal. _____
t'ward the west - ern star. _____

68

Additional lyrics

2. America's in motion
   And her hopes are a turnin' west.
   So let's all get a goin'
   For a new land's always best.

3. Oh, keep the bullwhips crackin'
   And a smile on ev'ry face.
   Keep the teams all pullin' even
   And each wagon in its place.

4. Now it's time to hold the wagons
   And circle for the night.
   Tomorrow roll the wagons
   When the sun is a shining bright.

When You Wish Upon a Star

from Walt Disney's PINOCCHIO

Words by Ned Washington
Music by Leigh Harline

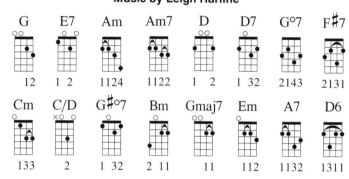

Whistle While You Work

from Walt Disney's SNOW WHITE AND THE SEVEN DWARFS

Words by Larry Morey
Music by Frank Churchill

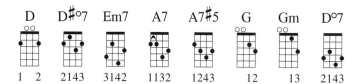

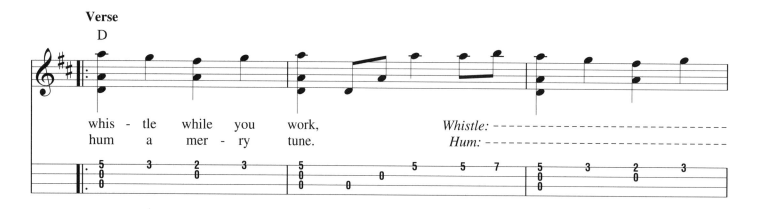

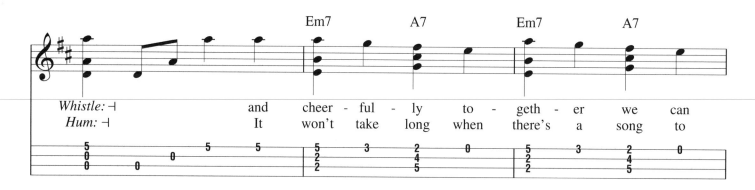

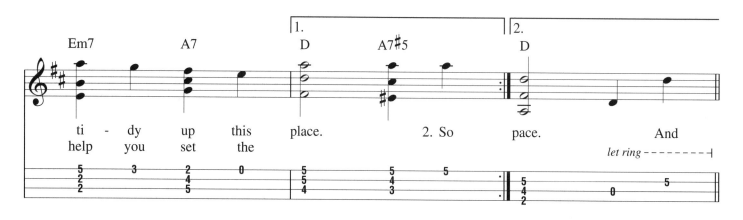

Bridge

G

as you sweep the room, im - ag - ine that the

let ring ------- *let ring* ------- *let ring* ------------------------ *sim.*

Gm

broom is some - one that you love, and soon you'll

D   D°7   Em7   A7   **Verse** D

find you're danc - ing to the tune.

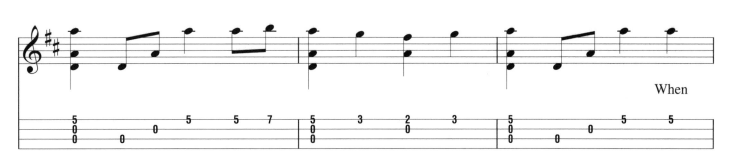

When

Em7   A7   Em7   A7   Em7   A7   D

hearts are high, the time will fly so whis - tle while you work.

You Can Fly! You Can Fly! You Can Fly!

from Walt Disney's PETER PAN
Words by Sammy Cahn
Music by Sammy Fain

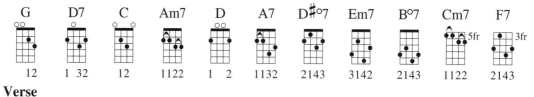

Verse
Lively

1. Think of the pres - ents you've brought, _____ an - y mer-ry lit-tle thought. _____
2., 3. *See additional lyrics*

Think of Christ - mas, think of snow, think of sleigh bells, here we go! Like

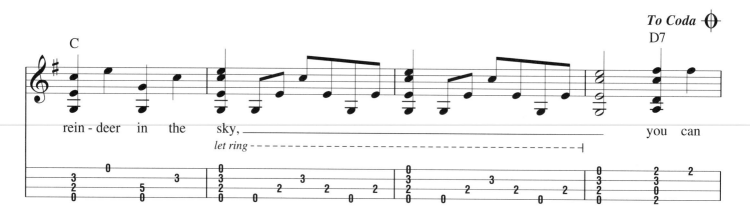

To Coda

rein - deer in the sky, _____ you can
let ring -

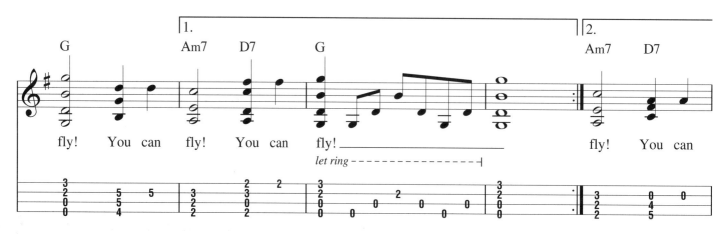

fly! You can fly! You can fly! _____ fly! You can
let ring - - - - - - - - - - - - - - -

Bridge

fly! _____ Soon you'll zoom all a - round the room, all it

takes is faith and trust; but the thing that's a pos - i - tive must _____ is a

let ring - - - -| *let ring - - - - -|* *let ring - - - -|*   *let ring - - - - - - - - - - - - - -|*

D.C. al Coda

lit - tle bit of Pix - ie Dust. _____ The dust is a pos - i - tive must.

let ring - - -| let ring - - - -| *let ring - - - -|*

𝄌 Coda

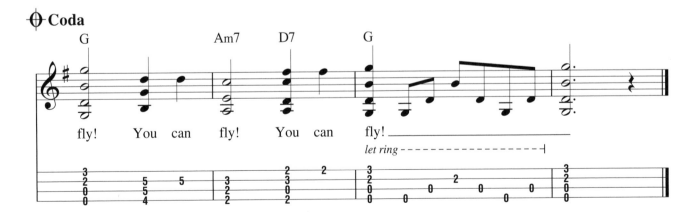

fly! You can fly! You can fly! _____

let ring - - - - - - - - - - - - - - -|

Additional Lyrics

2. Think of the happiest things,
That's the way to get your wings.
Now you own a candy store.
Look! You're rising off the floor.
Don't wonder how or why.
You can fly! You can fly! You can fly!

3. When there's a smile in your heart,
There's no better time to start.
It's a very simple plan,
You can do what birdies can;
At least it's worth a try.
You can fly! You can fly! You can fly!

Zip-A-Dee-Doo-Dah

from Walt Disney's SONG OF THE SOUTH

Words by Ray Gilbert
Music by Allie Wrubel

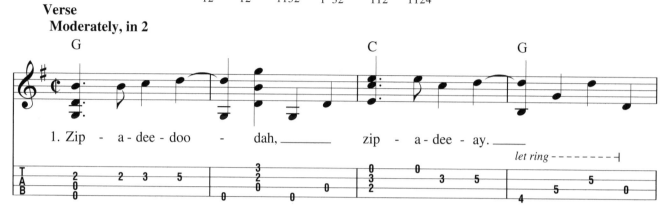

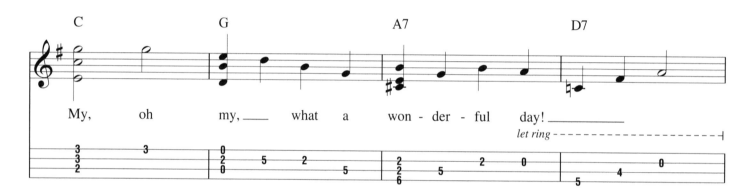

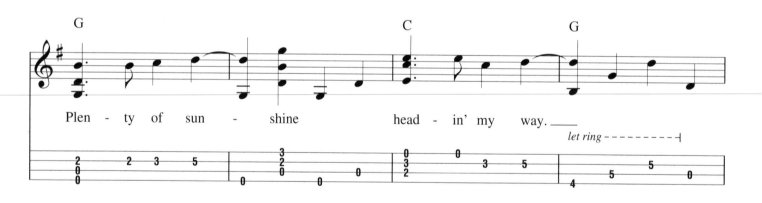

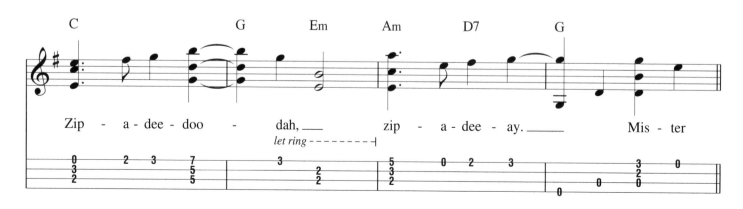

Bridge

Blue - bird on my shoul - der. _____ It's the

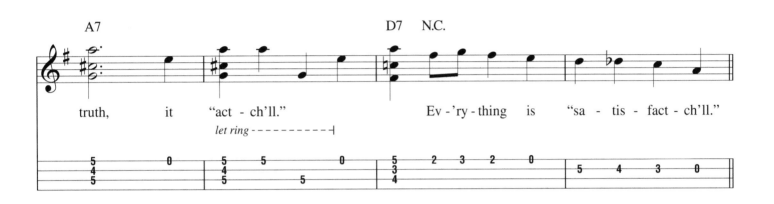

truth, it "act - ch'll." Ev -'ry - thing is "sa - tis - fact - ch'll."

let ring - - - - - - - - -

Verse

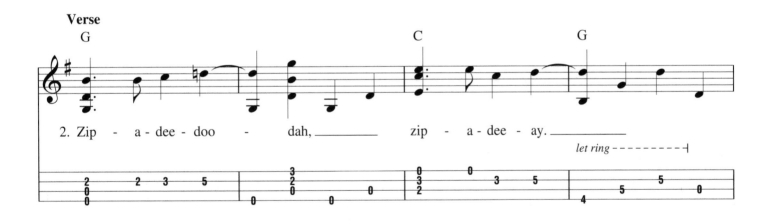

2. Zip - a - dee - doo - dah, _____ zip - a - dee - ay. _____

let ring - - - - - - - - -

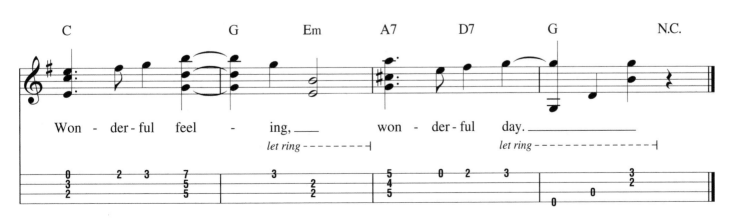

Won - der - ful feel - ing, _____ won - der - ful day. _____

let ring - - - - - - - -   *let ring - - - - - - - - - - - - - - -*

Who's Afraid of the Big Bad Wolf?

from Walt Disney's THREE LITTLE PIGS
Words and Music by Frank Churchill
Additional Lyric by Ann Ronell

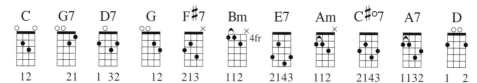

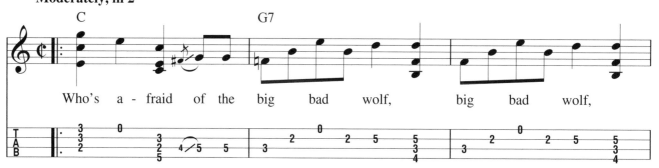

Chorus
Moderately, in 2

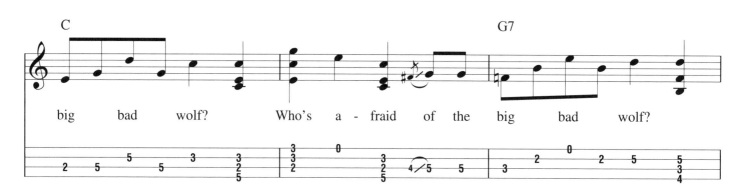

Who's a-fraid of the big bad wolf, big bad wolf,

big bad wolf? Who's a-fraid of the big bad wolf?

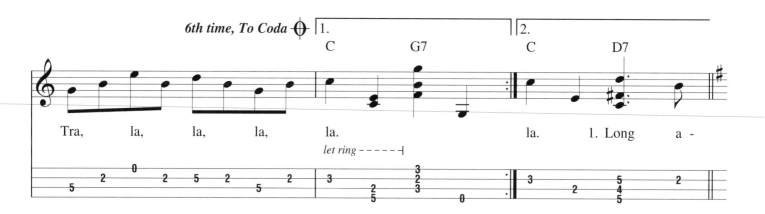

6th time, To Coda ⊕

1.

2.

Tra, la, la, la, la.   la.   1. Long a-

let ring

Verse

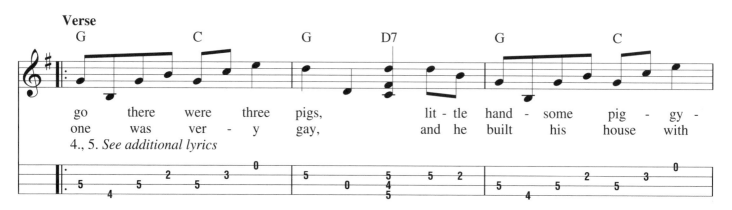

go there were three pigs, lit-tle hand-some pig-gy-
one was ver-y gay, and he built his house with
4., 5. See additional lyrics

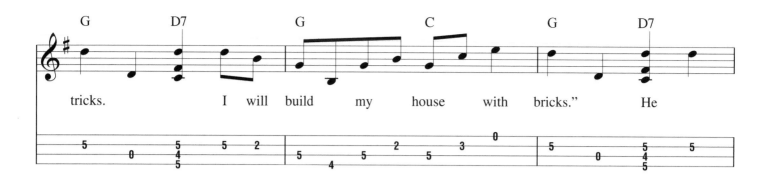

tricks.   I   will   build   my   house   with   bricks."   He

had   no   chance   to   sing   and __ dance 'cause _ work   and   play   don't

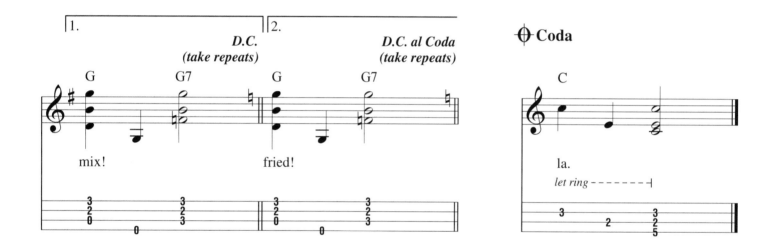

mix!   fried!   la.

Additional Lyrics

Verse 4   Came the day when fate did frown
             And the wolf blew into town.
             With a gruff "puff, puff" he puffed just enough,
             And the hay house fell right down.

Verse 5   One and two were scared to death
             Of the big bad wolfie's breath.
             "By the hair of your chinny-chin I'll blow you in."
             And the twig house answered, "Yes."

Bridge 2 No one left but number three
             To save the piglet family.
             When they knocked, he fast unlocked
             And said, "Come in with me!"

Verse 6   Now they were all safe inside,
             And the bricks hurt wolfie's pride.
             So he slid down the chimney and oh, by Jim'ny,
             In the fire he was fried!